The Wright Brothers

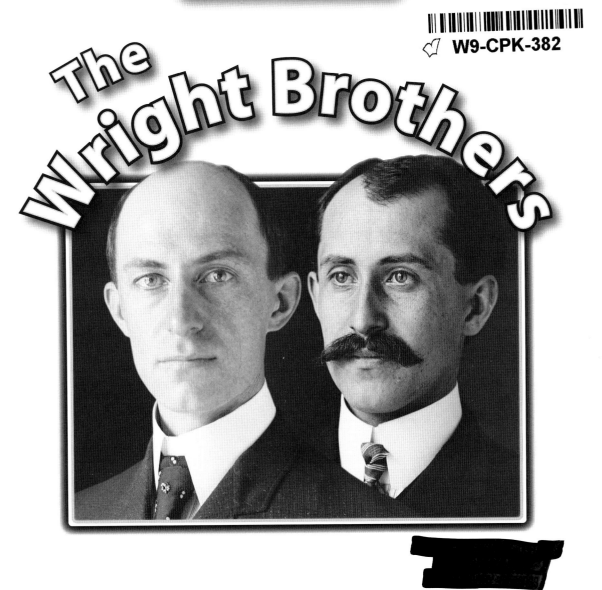

by Jonatha A. Brown

Reading consultant: Susan Nations, M.Ed., author/literacy coach/consultant

WEEKLY WR READER®
EARLY LEARNING LIBRARY

Please visit our web site at: www.earlyliteracy.cc
For a free color catalog describing Weekly Reader® Early Learning Library's list
of high-quality books, call 1-877-445-5824 (USA) or 1-800-387-3178 (Canada).
Weekly Reader® Early Learning Library's fax: (414) 336-0164.

Library of Congress Cataloging-in-Publication Data

Brown, Jonatha A.
 The Wright brothers / by Jonatha A. Brown.
  p. cm. — (People to know)
 Includes bibliographical references and index.
 ISBN 0-8368-4314-2 (lib. bdg.)
 ISBN 0-8368-4321-5 (softcover)
 1. Wright, Wilbur, 1867–1912—Juvenile literature. 2. Wright, Orville, 1871–1948—Juvenile
literature. 3. Aeronautics—United States—Biography—Juvenile literature. 4. Aeronautics—
United States—History—Juvenile literature. I. Title. II. People to know (Milwaukee, Wis.)
 TL540.W7B734 2004
 629.13'0092'273—dc22
 [B]   2004044478

This edition first published in 2005 by
Weekly Reader® Early Learning Library
330 West Olive Street, Suite 100
Milwaukee, WI 53212 USA

Based on *The Wright Brothers* (Trailblazers of the Modern World series) by Gretchen Will Mayo
Editor: JoAnn Early Macken
Designer: Scott M. Krall
Picture researcher: Diane Laska-Swanke

Photo credits: Cover, title, pp. 13, 15, 19 © Library of Congress; p. 5 © Bettmann/CORBIS;
pp. 6, 7, 9, 11, 16, 17 Courtesy of Special Collections and Archives, Wright State University;
p. 12 © Hulton-Deutsch Collection/CORBIS; p. 20 © CORBIS

Printed in the United States of America

1 2 3 4 5 6 7 8 9 08 07 06 05 04

Table of Contents

Words that appear in the glossary are printed in **boldface**
type the first time they occur in the text.

Chapter 1: Boys and Their Toys

The Wright brothers were born more than 130 years ago. In those days, people did not live the way we do now. They burned wood and coal to heat their homes. When they needed light, they lit a gas lamp or a candle. They did not have phones, TV sets, or cars. People could only dream of machines that fly through the air.

The Wrights came from a large family — four boys and a girl. They lived in Dayton, Ohio. Wilbur, the quiet one, liked reading and math. His brother Orville — Orv, for short — was four years younger. He was active, and he liked all kinds of **gadgets**. Orv always wanted to know what made things work.

The two boys were best friends. They shared ideas as easily as they shared toys and hobbies.

Loving Parents

Orv and Will's mother was very good with her hands. She built toys for her children. Once she even made a sled for them. When the children broke something, she showed them how to fix it.

Mr. Wright was a minister. He liked to bring home toys that made his children think. He wanted the kids to ask questions and find their own answers.

This picture is from the 1800s. It shows an idea for a flying machine.

Once he gave Orv and Will a whirling toy that floated and spun in the air. The boys liked it very much.

Wilbur Wright was born on April 16, 1867. He was twelve when this picture was taken.

They were puzzled by it, too. They tried to figure out how that little toy worked. They called it "the bat."

This picture shows Orville Wright when he was eight years old. Orville was born on August 19, 1871.

Chapter 2: Young Men

Will was a good student all through high school. In 1885, he was almost ready for college. Then an accident changed his plans. It happened during a game of ice hockey. Someone took a wild swing, and a hockey stick hit Will in the face. His front teeth were knocked out.

Pain and Sorrow

Will was in great pain, and he did not heal quickly. He stayed in the house and read books. He also took care of his mother, who had fallen ill. Will nursed Mrs. Wright for three years, but she did not get better. She died on July 4, 1889.

After Mrs. Wright died, Orv did not want to go back to school. He wanted to go to work. He and a friend had worked with printing presses. Orv asked Will to join him in a printing business. Will agreed to be Orv's partner.

Susan Wright was Will and Orv's mother.

The two brothers built a printing press from scraps. They began printing a weekly newspaper. They called it the *West Side News*. A year later, they started a daily paper. It was called the *Evening Item*. Will was the editor. At the same time, Will and Orv ran a printing shop.

The paper did not last long. There were too many papers in the area. Will and Orv were ready for a new idea.

A New Start

In 1892, Orv bought a bicycle. Will bought one a few weeks later. Orv loved racing. Will liked to go for long rides in the country.

Both brothers liked working on bikes, too. Next to their printing shop, they opened a bike shop. There they built new bikes and fixed old ones.

Will and Orv's bike shop was in this building.

Chapter 3: Big Challenges

This was an early glider. It helped people learn about flight.

The bike shop did well. As Will grew older, though, he grew bored. He was very smart, and he liked working on big problems. He began to think about flying. Many men had tried to build a machine that could fly under its own power. Some had died trying. Why, he wondered, had they failed? What problems still had to be solved?

Will began asking questions. He wrote letters to men who had tried to build flying machines. The men wrote back. Soon Orv started asking questions, too. He and Will read and studied. They talked and talked. They decided to run some **experiments**.

A big gust of wind wrecked this glider.

The Wrights built a kite first. Kite building was not new to them. Orv had built many kites as a boy. His kites had flown so well that he had even sold some. Now he and Will wanted to build a kite to learn something. They wanted to learn how to control a flying machine.

They built a huge kite with two sets of light, **flexible** wings. They attached wires to the wings. When the wind blew the kite into the air, Orv pulled on the wires. The kite dipped and soared as he pulled. He was controlling the flight!

Will and Orv built a glider next. A glider is a big kite that can carry a person. The men looked for a place to test it. They needed a high hill with steady wind. They needed a clear field to land in. Finally, they found the place — Kitty Hawk, North Carolina.

Testing the Glider

Orv and Will took the glider to Kitty Hawk in 1900. They flew it first as a kite. They made many test flights. Then Orv climbed on board.

This picture shows Orv and Will testing their first glider.

He and the glider took off. He could not **pilot** it well, but he landed safely. Then he and Will went home to Ohio. They still had problems to solve.

Orv and Will built this glider in the early 1900s. It flew very well. In this picture, Orv is aboard.

Chapter 4: Flying High

Will and Orv worked hard for the next two years. They tested wing shapes in a wind tunnel. They found the best wing design. Then they went back to Kitty Hawk with a better glider. It flew well, and the men learned to pilot it in all kinds of wind.

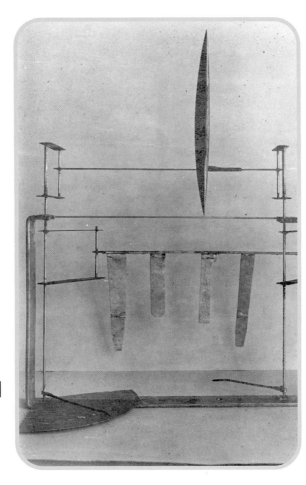

Orv and Will built this machine. They used it to test wing designs.

The Wright Brothers' Research

The shape of the wings affects how well a plane flies. A wing with the right shape gives a plane more lift. Lift is a part of the force that helps a plane rise.

The Wright brothers knew this. They wanted to make wings with good lift. They tested wing shapes in a wind tunnel.

They made a box with a fan at one end. On top, they put a window. They also made models of wing shapes called **airfoils**.

Then they tested the shapes. An airfoil was held in the box. The fan blew air across it.

The brothers tested many shapes and sizes. They looked for the ones that gave the most lift. It took a long time, but their research paid off. They found the best shapes for wings.

The next step was to add an engine and **propellers**. With the help of a friend, the brothers built both. Then they built a sturdy glider to carry the load. They called their new machine "the Flyer."

Orv and Will took the Flyer to Kitty Hawk in 1903. At first, storms kept them from testing it. Will tried to fly it once, but the wind was too strong.

Orv made history with this flight. The engine worked. The controls worked. The plane flew!

Orv and Will showed off for a crowd in 1909.

Orv's turn came on December 17. He set up a camera. The two brothers turned the propellers. When the engine started, Orv shook Will's hand. Then he climbed on board and pulled a lever. The wheels rolled over the sand, and the Flyer lifted up.

It rose off the ground. Someone took a picture. The bouncy flight lasted twelve seconds. Then Orv brought the Flyer back to Earth. Later that day, Will flew for almost a minute. The Wright brothers had made history!

Better Ideas

The two men flew over and over. They learned from every test. They kept trying new ideas. They built better flyers that stayed in the air longer and longer. Within a few years, Orv and Will Wright were known as the **inventors** of the airplane.

On December 17, 2003, the world honored the 100th **anniversary** of that first flight. We are no longer surprised to see machines that fly. People travel in jet planes and even spacecraft now. It all started with the Wright brothers. They made the dream of flight come true.

Glossary

airfoils — bodies such as airplane wings or propeller blades that push against air

anniversary — the yearly return of a certain date

experiments — tests

flexible — able to be moved or bent

gadgets — small machines or toys

inventors — people who make something for the first time. Inventors think about problems, use their imaginations, and test their ideas.

pilot — to fly an aircraft

propellers — blades that turn to move an airplane or ship forward

For More Information

Books

Big Book of Airplanes. Caroline Bingham (DK Publishing)

My Brothers' Flying Machine: Wilbur, Orville, and Me. Jane Yolen (Little, Brown & Company)

Taking Flight: The Story of the Wright Brothers. Stephen Krensky (Aladdin Library)

Web Sites

Dayton Metro Library

home.dayton.lib.oh.us/archives/wbcollection/wbphotos/wbphotos.html

Photos of the Wright Brothers, their family, and celebrations

U.S. Centennial of Flight Commission

www.centennialofflight.gov/media/photo/congress/display/1congress.htm

Photos of the Wright Brothers, Kitty Hawk, and more

Index

About the Author

Jonatha A. Brown has written several books for children. She lives in Phoenix, Arizona, with her husband and two dogs. If you happen to come by when she isn't at home working on a book, she's probably out riding or visiting with one of her horses. She may be gone for quite a while, so you'd better come back later.